ASSORTED POEMS

ASSORTED POEMS

SUSAN WHEELER

FARRAR, STRAUS AND GIROUX
NEW YORK

FARRAR, STRAUS AND GIROUX
18 West 18th Street, New York 10011

Grateful acknowledgment is made for permission to reprint excerpts from the
following previously published materials:
Poems from *Bag 'o' Diamonds* reprinted with the permission of the University
of Georgia Press.
Poems from *Smokes* reprinted with the permission of Four Way Books.
Poems from *Source Codes* reprinted with the permission of Salt Publishing.
Poems from *Ledger* reprinted with the permission of the University of Iowa
Press.
The poem "Reflected Sonnet" originally appeared in the exhibition catalog
April Gornik: Paintings and Drawings (New York: Edward Thorp Gallery,
2000).
The poem "In Sky" originally appeared in the exhibition catalog
Susanna Coffey: New Work (New York: Tibor de Nagy Gallery, 2001).

Library of Congress Cataloging-in-Publication Data
Wheeler, Susan, 1955–
     Assorted poems / Susan Wheeler. — 1st ed.
       p.   cm.
     ISBN-13: 978-0-374-25861-0 (hardcover : alk. paper)
     ISBN-10: 0-374-25861-9 (hardcover : alk. paper)
     I. Title.

  PS3573.H43465A9 2009
  811'.54—dc22

               2008053239

Designed by Gretchen Achilles

www.fsgbooks.com

10 9 8 7 6 5 4 3 2 1

TO MAX AND OSCAR

CONTENTS

BAG 'O' DIAMONDS

Bag 'o' Diamonds   3
The Grace That Is Sleep   4
What Memory Reveals   5
The Belle   7
Peanut Agglutinin   8
The Rudiments of Baublery   9
Journal of the Thousand Choices   11
Bankruptcy & Exile   13
The Privilege of Feet   14
Promoting the Restoration of Resilience   15
El, North & Milwaukee   17
Knowledge, Say   18
Private   21
The Man with the Green Card   22
Lasting Influence   23
Ruinous Disbelief   25
The Soul That Was Sister Carrie's   26
Debates   28
Here   Comes   Sparky   30
A Filial Republic   32
The Stable Earth, the Deep Salt Sea   34

SMOKES

He or She That's Got the Limb, That Holds Me Out on It 37
Rehearsal for The Breaks   ..   38
Beavis' Day Off   41
The Dogwood and the The   42

Ethic   43

Smokes   44

Ezra's Lament   46

Alphabet's End   48

Possessive Case   49

Invective: You Should Know   50

Song for the Spirit of Natalie Going   52

Shanked on the Red Bed   53

Meeting Again, After Heine   54

Sonnet of Alternate Starts for a Poem of Comparison   55

Run on a Warehouse   56

Fractured Fairy Tale   58

The View from There   59

Clock Radio   60

Chosen   61

SOURCE CODES

Self and Attributes   65

Fivers   67

Produce, Produce   69

Every Lover Admires His Mistress   70

The Promise of Steuben   72

Hand-Me-Downs: The Movies   75

Benny the Beaver: My Father's Tale   77

Rite Two: Two   79

Air Map   82

Guest + Host = Ghost   84

Sleeping Sister   85

Cassius   86

Quincy in Lagos   87

LEDGER

    Loss Lieder 91

    That Been to Me My Lives Light and Saviour 92

    Roanoke and Wampumpeag 95

    The Green Stamp Book 96

    Each's Cot an Altar Then 97

    Carnival 100

    Short Shrift 101

    Money and God 111

    The Debtor in the Convex Mirror 121

CATALOGS OF EXHIBITION

    Reflected Sonnet 139

    In Sky 140

    Acknowledgments *143*

BAG 'O' DIAMONDS

Denn schwer ist zu tragen
Das Unglück, aber schwerer das Glück.

For hard to bear is
Misfortune, but harder is fortune.

FRIEDRICH HÖLDERLIN, *"Der Rhein"*

BAG 'O' DIAMONDS

That there might be lines,
Or a plane which two lines make,
Or gold light, brown earth.

That this would be all there is,
That this would be enough to fill
The chest and cranium.

I did not know my family
When they looked in on me.
A silver sawdust come to roost.

I had one faculty too few,
Green shoes, laces blue.
A phrenologist could underrate.

That the plane the two lines make
Becomes the jar upon my nub,
The pin that keeps my rest with me.

Oh ye who considereth the faith,
Can ye slam the wong straight?

THE GRACE THAT IS SLEEP

There were two children, fuming around through the rooms of their
house that had much bric-a-brac to upset. It wasn't even raining,
although the other houses on the street were unnaturally quiet.
The children were unnerved together and sullen apart. They shut doors,
opened them again on each other with frantic laughing. The children
wanted something that was due the other so that each might rest.

This could have been the story I told you as you lay,
diving into dread, craving respite. This might have been
the story that unfastened, and lifted up for you,
an azure becoming sleep. But it is this voice that makes you
swoon: this story is one loosening tool listing into another,
each bearing its affects like wands, like tricksters' cups.
Sleep now: it is always in the telling, not the tale.

WHAT MEMORY REVEALS

Angels, pulled into light—provoking the air, fall
here. You are served a fallow breakfast;
you must stir your juice. Outside, on Columbus Avenue,
a momentary lunge convenes a trafficked burst.

This is not what was intended when they took you to your first
photo session, swaddled. But intent is a ruinous composite.

There were several years of careful steps across
lower Manhattan. A looming sail in a nightmare,
a poolhall, crisscrossed by rudimentary reliefs.
Mayonnaise in a refrigerator door.

You stepped forward, into light, onto a green lawn dotted with tumblers
and the hum of Minnesota cicadas. Everywhere a firm rejoinder waved.
He whispered the simplest, the pettiest of comforts. Your dress alit.

A fat man bends beneath the beaker's proximity.

Freakish, the two that burst into your room where you
were gathering privacy frantically, phonetically.
Burnish (they are flying) *regulation* (appointments a
calamity of rosewood)—or perhaps they said
furnish the nation. This left a hole, that left a lacking,
and he, the dog, had it, too.

Now Thalia rearranges the glove compartment.
On the right there is a quiet flapping, a whirring
or a wheel joint, in a bright and terrifying night.

It was time that altered monster genes. Pressed to the rear of a
new elevator toward a model apartment, you started with the sail,
with the tremoring that troubles you still. Like the murderer
who only dreamed, you can't shake catastrophe's history.
Your cuff, straightened now, is white against your suit.
The cordialities confirm.

Diving into water his wings conflated. Business
is damage.

What have you pricked, a tourniquet hamstring
under a revolver of lights?

A Lone Ranger replies. There is a waffling like a tournedos
of bundled wings. An egg drops out.

You pay for your breakfast and its litaneutical menu,
scrambled.
There is earth enough to fill each car,
each open mouth yawing in the light
on Columbus Avenue.

THE BELLE

Sad, that *porking* verb. I went down
With the fancy dyke to the parts store then
And that Billy crafted up a neurasma
Like as not the bends. *Nice legs.*

Felicity, a mom that's got a skittish grin
For every time the car door slams.
Come again: coquette off, on, and when
That lady turns her eye on you depends.

A girl labels each excretion in a box.
Mom's beat. (I'd like to say the tigers
Then the fear a far cry from complete.)
Come gently, wash those *hi-boys* here.

PEANUT AGGLUTININ

The gore being chili sauce and rice didn't mitigate
the way she died. Done in,
curtain furled at sunset then, the cat arced
and sped off behind the Donut Hut and we
see against the tar curbside one lone foot splayed.
And what a plan it was, though most missed the boat—
this way to the sawmill, inspector!

Nell too fell victim to his terrible design.
Out in the ever woods where the tree trunks stood
the blood seeped from plastic bags
and the crew had to make another ketchup run.
Lissa was tired of peeling grapes for eyeballs,
and Buck of scooping mayonnaise into insulated gloves.

Yeah, well here's what she liked: hair, and lots of it,
peanut brittle—when suddenly, a frost of cicadas,
rising like Lucifer, hums up the clouds—an
evening beside you: Do-right, do right again.

THE RUDIMENTS OF BAUBLERY

SETTINGS

A certain fascination with others' undressing
persists for years. Yours, for instance,
husks from a green stalk.
Everyone counts down. Everyone looks for
the signs of dénouement.
Everyone is more the mystery you lack.

PEARLS

The lights make for a veritable marquee
and, under the awning, the girl watches
with a pernicious aplomb.

ONYX

Like mercury. It is all like mercury, in the
late afternoon, liquid, on the steps
leading to the institution. Someone
bicycles by; Anita waves.
Your eyes are like liquid, looking up,
mercury suspended in tar.

RUBIES

The parking lot is tremulous with voices.
Before you get the knack of it, you are

asked to resolve certain of their questions.
What night? What girl?
What was the whispering on the edge of each joke?
This must be what you missed! You turn
the flat coin twice in your hand.
A telephone nearby rings.

SAPPHIRE

The rapt dogma of wonderment
prevails. A wand, a wisp of a girl
steps from the darkened room onto the
carpet of the suburban theater.
How slight these crossings are,
weaving between bodies a light,
dismarauding a desert.

JOURNAL OF THE THOUSAND CHOICES

I   DINNER

So that's what you've got in your back pocket.
Come over here. And when she moves to her left
the Missouri courthouse behind her looms into view until
you are distracted by her collar, alive as it seems.

II   JOB

The acacia at the bayou bloomed a thousand times,
a thousand times. A small librarian
born to better things sang I see the moon and the moon
sees me. The townspeople, caught off guard, watched
the lobe suspiciously. The tower tolled a dozen chimes —
it tolled for thee.

III   RELATIONS

She wanted burgers but before they had even hit the grill
a police car pulled up in front of the restaurant and two cops bolted in
with fire arms out.

IV   CITY & STATE OF ORIGIN

Land in malachite, eyeball the sediment, stratify the
limonite. What breather breaks the chert, the flint?
What arrow bursts obsidian? I have a dollar bub
the pyrite rains round here like gold.

V   CANNED GOODS

Lassia found her skating and skating around
the Tyrolean pond in circles. Herr Settembrini
had but just left her,
and Lassia became shy at her new ruddiness.
The words alarmed at the larynx,
the steam of the blade on the ice,
the rise of the fruit at her chest,
the falling of water, the roar.

Here, unwrap the cigar and cut it like so.

VI   SCHOOL

Châteaubriand this, châteaubriand that.
Like pekinese sniffing at table,
Mr. Lewis and his electric organ spun
the stuff of a thousand halls.

BANKRUPTCY & EXILE

Along the horizon, the exhausted buildings tilt above
the darkened streets. This silence means
a tarnishing of trade. Before you step into the gaunt
alley, your hand releases a periapt of hope.

Divisions when agreements rent come. This dappled beast
in green finds fault with the quietest prudences, uses the
sword you left behind to hack away at social convocations.
There is no calling for the dream is wavering.

Then the cloud that made the kitchen dark passes.
She is turning the leaves of the magazine and laughing.
She is knowing the silent parting of the skin that soothes the heart.

A crater appears beside the trees, in the dark.
The line that means horizon bends beneath the moon.

THE PRIVILEGE OF FEET

Superb wandering this:
glacier unfed by light,
the object of fidelity,
or the azure wildflower, bending.
It is not so much embellishment,
this reasoning into language.

His first word was *breakfast*, his
second *porridge*. Then he learned
to mate two halves of a
limonite concretion on a shelf.
His Tigers' cap
brushed against his glasses.
He tried peeing
in the sink,
from the top of the toilet seat.
He called geology
jeedocy.

And does this fabric account for
the fiction of family? Too many
highballs. Too much sun.

The starboard tack arrested
the brunt of the luffing, and
several careful swimmers
took a dive, thinking nothing
of the decorative this became:
headfirst, a word
described as *festive*.

PROMOTING THE RESTORATION OF RESILIENCE

A world is arranged for this, she thinks,
counting the cups which have fallen to the floor.
Autumn on Route 7 brings truckers.
Now a gust follows one in; beyond the lot
there lies a wood waving frantically, back and forth,
the lonely wag a man provides in bed.

And now Bob (for that is the trucker's name)
bobs his arm to eat his eggs, as the trees sway,
as Clarice imagines it so slow that breathing stops
and platters up the pieces that have broken.
A waft becomes a burning on the grill. What word,
she thinks, describes an invented noun? *Perfidy.*

The sense that it suffices is misleading freight:
beneath the truth a puddle forms, reddens.
Without the frantic storm this man would have been
miles from here, and his startling entrance mute,
these cups intact, the trees and Clarice's thoughts
still, swollen. The kicking sounds the children make
against the booth provoke another order then.

I could not find my father in the dunes, and in the
Chatham grass the sky became the flipped sense
of what this all would be if not for chance.
My brother stumbled by my side and clasped onto
the razor reeds that craftily made different
the sands I had learned were not once alike.
Or snowflakes—I was not sure; they both made
a whirling blindness out of purpose, and of praise.
This is what I learned about table manners, about

greeting the elderly, about ways to fold my socks.
Only blindness, only chance, and then a rule derives.

Wild undulations of the eulalia. The stand of elms
dares Clarice to rise and enter in: a stopwatch
in an unruly, billowing snow.
And by the time the trucker drives the last of egg
with toast, Clarice is sifting out the underbrush
of a wooded terrain.
Deft practices arise, and now a bird alights.

It was like all of this, that falling into dunes
or into waters which held small craft
like a beached and gargantuan bug, removed and
flicked onto a plaza in the rain. That
small semblance of the individual: the
quiet chewing, thoughtfully, which the grasshopper
brings to grass.

EL, NORTH & MILWAUKEE

A host is watching you, as you turn the bend,
a child come into an awesome puberty.
It is the nightshift off, at ten.
Nightly a gust ballasts them,
on this lea of lust, the ten orange men.

Walking, you must seal the seam of your desire
and this spring dream. You do, and theirs are there,
overtime: the calls, like red needles, raining;
the snowballs, after school, your brother made;
the dead assaults, up from the blue community arcade
preparing more. '*Ras*mus Johnson, leave the window.
The host shakes out the early evening shavings and
parts itself clean. Walking, you must bring
a way to breathe, to be afraid.

KNOWLEDGE, SAY

I

That forever describing experience,
on and on, the stuff of conversation,
forgetting to the last, losing it, unhinging,
until even the children leave answers—
for there they are, in the gazebo, twirling on
storks' legs, serving up wieners—

Those two in the masks, that found your heart beating
under the rock, did they know you wanted that dumb pencil,
biggest in the world, you lapping the interstate
tunnels like a tourist, in, out?
In the night air the piñon branch, torched to smell
like clover, illumined the tools at his waist;
they swung out gently as he stepped.
How had you known that by succumbing,
those hideous gnats would come in by the door?
And suddenly
the belly is rancid.

The archaeology is false, you know—
just what I have been telling you.
You let a cup fall from your roof—the pigeons swoop up
like your hair perhaps caught in this plastic comb.

II

What have you seen? Why doesn't this work?
Where are the answers now since I've plugged along

keeping my nose so clean?
When will you speak to me? What are you toying with?
Who are you waiting for, please?

The hut's window curtains waft, and before the bear rears
the gutter clangs. All at once, the silverware tarnishes
and tears out of there.

When will you let me rest? What will give me peace?
Why are the wheels spinning and the heads knocking
and the bees banging into the wall?
Where can I go to get to you? What is this, hide-and-seek?
When will these adamant choristers stop?

The man named Buster in the woodshop was no dog.
He knew what he was worth, he asked for it: an honest day's wage,
an honest day's work.

Why are these colleagues yammering so?
Why do you elude me? Where are you now?
What distance is there that makes you fathoms,
miles, acres away from me? Will you bring them back?
Will I see?

III

Yeah but how does it know? That Thermos,
there. After one or two of the outsiders—
No. Pretend it is Danny Kaye whispering about Tekla
from the red vinyl, and nowhere outside a leaf stirs

while Mom's in her office and the full sway of the afternoon
says *Hours. Fill them.*

I must have no inner resources because I am heavy bored—
His marker sinking to the bottom of the river
and his hat flying out across the used car lot—
the way that I have ever known. But for the. Lighting here.

PRIVATE

Extemporaneously the bird alit
and the door to the hovel swung in the rain.
The gnome put the child to bed. I swam.

The pool was as dark and as deep as a well,
and pine needles swelled its banks.
The skunk cabbage waved its odiferous brew.

My father stepped out on the pier in the rain.
I wanted you mightily, mightily home,
and the dogs tore in barking at night.

THE MAN WITH THE GREEN CARD

Tenderness becomes its own reflex, like the cradled
cup in the hands, or the random administration of frailty.
They eat grass bo, bo.
Felicity burns deeper than the merchandise it culls:
a fare bounty and a pygmy's dream.
Sometimes I eat grass, bo, bo.

Forge love: beyond the committee chambers
there lies a green field with buttercups and rodents
romping. Beyond the peculiar chaos of a dog's nails
on a tenement stair the body's ebullience requires ash.

The belt may not be a tautening creek for the land.
Eliciting fire, the keys in his fist, a faucet for indigence,
perfidious hire—they eat grass in the night, bo, bo,
fastening, fast, like this button that's pearl under flickering.

LASTING INFLUENCE

This is the repugnant part, where now
you covet the loss which a moment before
brought you the severed torso in the dream.
Since your friends are feasting, you must act quickly.
The child's carriage careens on the stair.

Dancing a rondo on the lacustrine tile,
you look up suddenly to a beveled undoing.

This is no respite or reward.

For so many years you have cast out, learning to
search (you think of roses), and now it is clear
that the driveway which borders this undulant lawn
is the twilight escape route of robbers. In another life,
they catch the children at the critical moment
and bundle the bodies from the cold.

The imagined wit, you think, is never worth the bargaining.

Then the plane takes off, and the woman with the poodle
snuffs your cigar and takes a brick from her purse
and lifts a train of somnolence from the seat.
You are drifting; she has bent your ear, singing;
you are under the wing of an implacable monster.
Grace is elephantine, it does not mean reward.

So you undid something unexpected, and in your delight
you forgot to inquire whether it was something reasoned
or only a precarious dish on a shelf. Possession become
indistinguishable, fireflies raffling on a screen,

a route of departures crossed like wires through which,
during hideous nights, voices make divisions of lives.
Each day you have locked a door and turned out a lamp
that brought only the sorriest comfort while lit.
Now the whole rift derives clearly.

She calls to say, she is ready to depart, is there anything
you need? Then it is you recognize the precipice
for what it is, then you see that out there, on the
dawning bridge of a fallacious jump, a cowboy is
coming after you, calmly askew, promising breath.

RUINOUS DISBELIEF

Sands, similitude, what's the difference?
I could use a stand-in but even this,
which seems to refer, makes a figure.
Despair does not well take representation.

Once they'd bedded the children,
there was a small reading by candlelight,
prayers and the scent of skin.
They did not always answer each other.

A sudden boost in the air-conditioning stiffens the air.
The bird that calls everyone Chuckie, eats.
I am going out to the mailbox now.

It was basically a kind of faith we had inherited,
after years of singing and then diving into roomfuls of
goofballs and their cars. Idiocy. Own to every stroke
that damages the waving, green-backed lawn.

Something will fall from the sky and into a sea nest.

Before he went into the arena, he stooped over the wooden
bucket, took up the oil and crossed himself.
There was a dry wind, broken by the seats on the east.
A few bums dozed lazily, stirring.
The coins in his shirt had worn the fibers thin.

Oh pocket it. But then the pocket grows. The boats
pull against strong tide. Words make a muck, and then
gestures—you might as well forget it, forget the drift.

You want to reply but the overture is over, and in the
snuffled silence the curtain creaks to either side
and Rusika with tinseled hair strides out.
In the waft of your wife's perfume the stage's flack
subsides, although her hand—on the armrest—waves
from Siberia. *I learned hemming from Miss Aggie,* says Rusika.

Coming down from the blue peak the mountaineer
stumbles, holding one finger around the aluminum catch
on a fragrant vest.
My friend Felicia offered him a bowl of crackers as a bribe.

And then the count, from the divan, unwinds and says
The hell with that shit. Beside you your wife shifts
with relief, she had said they were dweebs.
But after the party, when the streamers come down, you sit
next to the treasure chest and wail.
The basement is filled with chalk marks marking hopscotch.
From the stairwell swings the camping gear.

What did you care, that the strummings came to so little?
They wanted you so whole, so still, a whelp or two
from a stoop you only thought you remembered,
so clear was that daguerreotype.
In the midst of the leap Road Runner hit a pocket of air
which, glass, held him and then
dropped him off the bottom of the screen.

Billy had two baby gherkins and he split one up the middle,
saying, *First you take a H bomb*, writing,
I want a anorek (sp?), saying,
then that canned Kansas virtue,
but in the bucolic frenzy of the swallows
I'll tell you now I missed the rest.
The half crazed cowlick of a grebe fell into the Styrofoam.

And later when you'd wasted a life, the beat began.
The frenetic upholstery suddenly clashed with the scene
on the VCR; there were unbidden lumps in your linings;
I heard you humming a flimsy tune.

The cave in his chest, clear as a C print,
gleamed in the wax of the page.

DEBATES

Damn it Graw you've got the sponge
on the wrong side of the ketchup bottle.
Have not shithead. And thus we drift
like a loggering glacier
straightways into a century.
Hulk's crocheted a tissue box cover.
I pasted the floral decals on the soap.
Hey HONEY how 'bout some TLC?

It's only here beside the birdhouses
where Federica, Duchess of Ostheim,
plots in a pique, that the rotting birds re-
compose, assemble and then raise up
tailwards their bungling flocks.

Hester hadn't asked for anything more than that.
Collecting the *big* change had knocked the
wind out of her, and the thurifer had forgotten
a light. Day in, day out, an
infernal crumpling and exhaling:
the hay field in sudden illumination
or a malicious wave from the booth.

Even with sentinels, the ants are circling.
I asked you to wash up for dinner.

The orators clamped on their goggles and helmets
and then had another go. In kitchens men
turned to Lucy. The breakfasts once
imagined were lackluster now. And the
golden expansion was loose as a cannon
while the memory of promise mopped up.

Give me the hammer.
Hey wake up, bozo.
After all, other people had built—but now
the skipper rounds the bend, checks out shore,
and lumbers past to Circe. *Give it a rest willya*
and help me with this stripping. A girl winks from behind
a glass elevator chute.

Phil whispered with that superior look on her face.
One of the orators dropped his cigarettes, which as she knew
booted him out of the pie-throw routine.
Count to ten slowly. Don't break your stride.
Remember your affirmations, oh HP nation.
The nails now tumbling from the window ledge
each lodge when they fall behind an ear.

Vaudeville smoke, brains on fire, poppies
in the blue field beyond the great lawn,
deliberate dots on ice. The senses they forego,
stapling each thumb in place, for a long campaign.
I said the glue, dipshit. Oh come on here.

Second time around. Some greyhound, there,
reminds you of the hope you broke.
Becky and Bill filming in 1979, dead
pan. Bill's thinking and now he says:
Layer that gamelan at Get Ready, 'kay?
A hellish confluence, that's what it is,
and then it's up and attem with that
parcel of crackpots, chewing and grinning,
in the hellish breakfast room.

Maybe aural dynamics of some acetate film—

What you thought began at the river
When you undertook to select the stone
What you favored in the careful pummeling
How the bruise on the neck appeared.

She's found a fungus as large as a football
And before it thoroughly dries with a pencil she carves
Hades ain't for ladies.
The way the road looked.

Duped! All the high hopes you'd pinned on
Sparky's great fan, Silver Penny,
the dog's but a shadow of the horse, nonetheless:
poundage and age, lacking.
Everybody's Milton. Everybody's great.

On the drive he sang a western song:
> *Failing the bent and burgeoning drip*
> *Of the antifreeze on the engine mount,*
> *I'll bring you in, I'll bring you in.*

At the western sky the treacly sun declined.
Paul Harvey, buzzed in and out, along the
power lines in an august time,
while the arrow light on the motel marquee
faded at distance, in the dark.

Oh, get for real the Penny sings.

So how much of that dialogue will we borrow here,
after the man and the woman and the man trade places?
An overwrought Indian, over biryani and beer—
the belly up of garbage on Stony Island Boulevard—
the chunk of his arm which the notary redeemed—
the possibilities over the years we entertained!
We are signed on the backdrop that the choice we exacted
was clearly the cadaver's not ours.

You spread the papers now about the fiery sheets
and read the news.
It is a natural occasion.
It is an ordinary morning.
You are deranged as a plant is deranged
in a minefield of chlorophyll and gelignite,
training a leaf to the left.

A FILIAL REPUBLIC

. . . I sit
And smoke, and linger out desire.
ALVIN FEINMAN, *"November Sunday Morning"*

And out on the plaza, there were more people
Than had been expected: the aviators, with their
Thick dark muffs; the women in red, clapping
For Coca-Cola; the small trumpet player,
Leaning on the fender of the car which was not his;
The mechanics, spreading flat the manuals
For timing and for gaps; the blue majorettes;
The mother, who wished so hard she broke in two;
Those divided against the rule; Mick Jagger;
The security-green police; the gentle inquisitor;
The woman who had not yet found the voice for tragedy;
The exercise cadet, with Adidas and cassettes;
The deaf man, elegant, who bends to tie
His shoe; the grocery clerks, hanging back,
Aloof; the girls who clutched their T-shirts
From behind; the model with the cordless telephone;
The guests of honor, in their limousine;
The *New Yorker* hack; the derelicts, smitten with their
Own advice; the shampooer; the plasterer; the
Dishwasher; the drunk; the man so sodden with sex
He reeled; the crook; the benevolent sister;
The priest, wistfully; Allen Funt;
The father, crying with desire; the great
Conquistadors; the dreamers, who looked past the crowd
As it rolled in the sun; the children:
Exclaiming together, as one hut and then another,
South, on the horizon, burst into fire.

Rise up, from where you are seated, smoking,
At a wooden desk. There has been a terrible dream
In the apartment above you, and the tenant is pacing.

THE STABLE EARTH, THE DEEP SALT SEA

After the dark and in the quaking
the candles on the lawn go out.
You make a path across the slate like a snail.
Everybody spooks.

Duo Seraphim clamabant, alter ad alterum.
What whistling comes from within the trees,
from the bushes there that bend beneath
the breezes?

There were children on the lawn barely walking.

Plena est omnis terra. And you were divided
like wells and like windows, as access to a thing
you represent. Take what regret allows and go
toward light.

Many years ago the woman watched the child
from the stoop. The doorknob broke, and then—

Whom shall I send? And who will go for us?
Then I said, *Here am I! Send me.*

SMOKES

HE OR SHE THAT'S GOT THE LIMB,
THAT HOLDS ME OUT ON IT

The girls are drifting in their ponytails
and their pig iron boat. So much for Sunday.
The dodo birds are making a racket
to beat the band. You could have come too.

The girls wave and throw their garters
from their pig iron boat. Why is this charming?
Where they were nailed on their knees
the garters all rip. You were expected.

The youngest sees a Fury in a Sentra
in a cloud. This is her intimation and she balks.
The boat begins rocking from the scourge
of the sunset. The youngest starts the song.

REHEARSAL FOR *THE BREAKS*

I

He was WHACKED with religion.
And he was trying yea so mightily
not to sound spoonfed, he,
a cynical man,
educated to 30.

I GOT no ongoing circumstances.
He sinks upon the velvet seat
and codes the program back
in fribbling s'rrows.
A burning fire shut up in my bones—

II

After a sort of amiable striding-about the posy-snippers stop
at the edge of the audience and doff their shoes. They are not
sure what makes the crowd so high-strung and brittle tonight.
They are too far back to see the gameboard and point-of-play.

III

No no no, THAT Francis Bacon.
Is this his own voice, this
twirling and trafficked, gnarly
thing? What in the end
would his mother have said

hearing dicta to rival her own,
dangling the glorious bag
empty of chips in the
crackled sun? She might have
thought him snoring.

IV

They've had it with the hamstrung one. It's at a tricky point, where
traditionally six glass marbles sweep the board and end up in
Welsh Rarebit sauce. (*She* prefers ketchup on Saltines, but
heat it. The marbles crack from hot to ice.)
The wiggly crowd near the wisteria inhales and holds its breath.
The shooters are cued for the poof-in, to begin pummeling like rain.

V

Instead of your going
horsewires you can just say
"Chia needed somethin'" awright?
Chia! Y'know—chia pet! What
gentleman there is within thy wire scratching—

That voice again. He could deep-six
the lot of 'em, that risible lead
in his floppy tam, the starlet whose
pudenda pendulums before Tab A inserts.
His jangled nerves deliberate.

VI

This was the last word I was going to peel for you. You watch cars out
the window as you chew, and I try to explain before you're through
where last I saw the vocabulary. Stage left, before the mongering crew
gave the multitudinous audience a shoo and from then on out
it was cash & carry. No one's interest got furthered today.

VII

It's grace that's given them this
smoker of a grand design,
this man so WHACKED he stokes
the script with rewrites palmed unto
the hapless stand-in scripter, she,

a mistrust of loquacity, a finger
flecked with 'raser threads, an
impedimented personality.
That was my plan for him, hubristically.
A reclamation of sorts, after sodden reprieve.

BEAVIS' DAY OFF

He'd been doing a lot of cull-twanging,
he thought, walking back and forth on the deck
of his battleship—*whoa! correction*: loft.

Small fires burned on the outskirts of Soho;
Fanelli's lit up under a stickered sky:
cirrus pitched to the top of its firmament.

How long could he crimp the diesel in the dark?
The bedlam was breathing its own air now;
the parrot shivering in the freezer glared at the hen.

Please it's time said Meg. And each infernal
truism struck a package deal for tin.

What hast thou, O nut job, with paradise?
The sparks O they crested the floor then they floated
and she lay down on fine braids and she cried.

THE DOGWOOD AND THE THE

And in the center of the outer edge of each petal there
will be nail prints, brown with rust and stained with
red, and in the center of the flower will be a crown of
thorns, and all who see it will remember . . .
— *from various postcards, "The Legend of the Dogwood"*

The dazzling platters of the many-armed man,
The hundred plates spinning on the hundred spun fingers,
A trick whip *Step ON it you* soft in the skim of your skin—

The eye becomes inured to gaud. The bellicose kids fort up
The grand screen. *Cool, summa, wahm in the winta—*
Hey asshole! Take ya stringy hair out! The quarter's in,

The blip's on Calvary, the lamps of the memory palace under
Glass blink up at Ig. They were each a dipsy-doodle at heart
And the night washed in like ink. *Summer bun it drive me*

Crazy. And he said, *prosper beneath the blue water tank.*
And they said, *the fugger got it on hisself.* And I said,
Wait in the glen. A minute so I. Catch up wif you.

The tree don't know from passion. A stun gun blusts and
Blood scats in the glass, one player beating with his fist in time—
There has been a casualty. The bereaved will have their needs.

ETHIC

Manman got a special s'rup 't cures the lonelies.
All the night, up the tree'f the pickling shed
Ise drinking from it elixir.

Afters the sunup the hacked meat it come.
The truck it seethes on it brakes and the driver he look.
Ise swinging from t'friendly tree.

Then it smote. What business was mine
in the cardboard rune, in the native rap?
I on the tree stump, I missing all.

SMOKES

after James Schuyler

At the Chelsea Hotel, you sat on the edge of the bed while he rummaged
through drawers for cigarettes. The wind set by a big tumult at the glass.
Scrafing the view, the lone plane tree scissored an arm and subsided.
Suppose he had at that moment put his hand on your arm and said *Ethan*.
You would have had to have told him this was not your name, that indeed
you know no Ethan, Ethan may be an actor but what writer was Ethan,
and hadn't he summoned you here? In Washington they called them
redbuds, what was in bloom. Besides, suppose instead of correcting him
you had finally reached into your pocket for Luckys, had offered him a
Lucky, and his gratitude and relief were discernible in the slight gesture
he would make for you to wait while he found the poem. On the way in,
you had just seen a small girl in a flat halter jumping at you from the stair.
"Can you imagine planting redbuds in front of a brick house?" the Virginia
intellectual asked. Beyond the glass the light and the wind were becoming
Peter Brooks' storm scene from King Lear. Suppose then that he found the
sheet of paper that he was looking for and with Buddha's frown if Buddha
frowned he inhaled from the Lucky and the left corner of his lips rose as he
read over silently the poem, and then settled beside you on the bed taken
without giving any indication with your raven hair, your nervous laugh.
Suppose then he said, *Ethan, here it is. To live! To live!* he would read,
watching you without seeming to. The forsythia bursts out first with the
first single-headed daffodils; they riot with fire. In Atlanta, these have
long come and gone by now. Suppose all of this happened, and this attention
was really there. Suppose he attended to the delicacy of your attention.
Suppose he was a good mom, suppose he didn't brush your arm with his arm.
The sky darkened so quickly that the plane tree appeared spooky.
A siren scrawled a wail down 23rd Street that made it impossible to speak,
in the room. You took this opportunity to light another Kool and
saw your hands shake although you were young. Suppose with the brush
of his arm it was difficult to follow the poem but it was a poem to die for,

all of the nouns lined up and fascinating. Suppose he said, *Ethan, what
do you think?* There was a time when johnny jump-ups preceded forsythia,
the good old days. Evolution was the driving force behind the leapfrogging.
Everyone had assumed you had meant something different than you did,
afterwards, when you gave your account of the room. You saw the spring
as though beyond a shutting door. The older poems—I mean by centuries—
have given us enough time to really love them. Suppose you had responded
with unmediated admiration. Suppose then: *So Ethan, where are yours?*
After you lit the Kool and the siren fell you heard over the racket of the wind
a child running outside the door. A ladyslipper in a Stroh's bottle by the bed
made you think of Gloria Swanson in her last days, waxy and semi-trans-
lucent, speckled brown on green. He poured himself another Coke.

Suppose then that under the ginkgo on Mercer Street when the storm's
lid had latched he had said *Come with us Ethan why don't you?* The young
at the least can decorate. This would have been like the Santa Maria,
bumping the lap of the East Hampton pier, waiting its turn for a roll. Night
air whooshed the opaque, lit wall. You waited for this, and he didn't.
The redbud's a small tree, a scrapper, an adamant. Some are strong, some
weak, some like you with the breath of forgiveness cupping to light a Kool.

for David Trinidad

EZRA'S LAMENT

I owed the baker three dollies with heads.
I owed the singer a way to recoup.
I owed the bookmaker my mother's own sauce.
I owed the outfielder plenty, plenty.

I owed the swimmer a new way of speech.
Lucky I was that the view of the villa
Prevented my pitching the book overboard.
I owed the industrialist pinafore threads.

I owed the waters drops from my lenses,
I owed the bereaved, I owed a tiger,
A dentist, a hobbyist, a smallish crook,
The maîtresse d'hôtel—the shiniest stones.

What breath employs me thats salary should be
Paid in tenders I don't understand?
The bankruptcy makes ichnites of heirlooms
Strung across oxidized fiberboard pegs.

I owed Winslow a flowering grove, a bower.
I owed a simpleton plenty, plenty.
I owed the gentlest of Barbie collectors
A wracked afflicter and a soupçon of sand.

Machinate carefully, o if you should go there,
Clicking the debts like a rotary phone
Where the lifeline is sparked in the vectors.
That frantic believing will break you in two.

I owed who raised me the still of my back,
The television's glint in the model set store,
And I owed my brother a bike.
I owed the fence these Colorform 'toons.

The parch in the Playland is criminogenic.
I owed the insects swarming the creditors
Their own salt hearts, brittling the trees.
The army, and air force, plenty I owed.

O if you should go there in your twenty years
Remember the wank that you cannot repay,
O if you should, there in your twenty years.

ALPHABET'S END

So I'll speak ill of the dead. A was crooked,
planting the small left finger of the raccoon in the upholstery
before he sold the car. B made certain to point out Celia's
bewildered look before her pink slip came in the flimsy institution.
In the videos of C, a jejune overwhelmed the cast.

D built dollhouses. Even Lonnie down at Shell
found him less a man for it, the night they went off to see the stock
cars break. I wanted E's hair, but by the end it was no more. F
refused alms, pulling the man up by his shirt in the street, and
G sought rewards. Marybeth said H fondled her for sport.

Now you, I, Smokey, hell
bent on a village version of Club 21, embarrassed by our attentions.
Mistrust it was. Dig me a chamber of preparedness.

William T. Osborn, 1964–1993

48

POSSESSIVE CASE

What are you walking the hamjammies for.
It's always the same argument. The man scrapes
the molt from his forearm and cringes.

The scabs become virulent in their saucer.
The man harnesses their latent energy.
The man continues to prick, pick at the girl.

Seven flight suits are pounding at the door.
Words pound from seven visors. The words
fall in the saucer and make a molten pot hash.

The marquee in the saucer draws waterbugs.
Their inelegant eyebrows make needles for the girl.
He *might* have been capable of love. Worth trying.

The giant engine with its pistons of lamb arms
glides down their street on its skis. The pilots
use their balcony for streamers. Cheers.

Scabrous wasn't such a big deal. Where's the oven?
Under the spreading oak tree a steel filament blew.
He puts his johnson in his pants and begins to stew.

INVECTIVE: YOU SHOULD KNOW

ONE

Now you are in a lather over their taking the Scrabble pieces and using them for decoration. Refresh yourself, bone up on organizational skills, *a three-ring binder and this new version of Whist will fit you out like new.* For they are beginning to talk when you bend to tie your shoe. They say, *the 'x' goes perfectly in this xylophone.* Before the Roman with the brogue begins his hatcheting, you will have draped yourself as a workhorse courtesan with plenty of extra letters to spare. You will have blanks for everyone, on demand. They will know *just how invaluable you are: their burgeoning pockets will attest to it.* So now, wipe the spittle from your rouged chin. The players are waiting for you.

TWO

I knew my hand was not a valued commodity since I could not bring a powerful or even compelling family to it. It started with your dad's sweater, *that wonderful Italian cut,* watching you carried away by the romance of your dancer dad. Well it wasn't just *your* romance, everyone it seemed had a way of embellishing a family or in-laws—except perhaps for the thoroughly jaundiced, like mom, who didn't like anyone but the chirpy and anxious "helpers." It started when you held out the sweater and said, *Here it's my father's, it's a wonderful Italian cut, you can borrow this.* Suddenly all the Vegas motifs to the apartment lent you, the bearer, a tragic kind of 20th-century captive of sleaze giant kind of thing, dangling the Italian cut sweater from your outstretched arm.

THREE

In the meeting room your chaps, Festus, seemed out of place. How sunnily you seem to find the file tab that attaches to each article in seven. There was some talk among us studio sausages that you had run aground on the Foreign Correspondence project and canned the rest, and that is why you hum to yourself at table. Yesterday I saw your wife picking peaches into your rival's basket—she had the softest smile, like strawberries, hell-bent on your ruin.

FOUR

I hadn't forgotten the favor you had done me in the barn catercorner to the milk-pond those some ten years ago, and when that peacenik spoke ill of you I rose to your defense. I told him about your cock, dear heart, about the wiggle in its walk and the soft cradle you made of the down for my head. If I mentioned the leg you ran off with, my only steed, if I happened to say that the books you were selling could not substitute, if I said that your fingers were as fast and my fall as great as Lucifer's, that you and I are much alike, that His Will it was and His Will is cruel, if the peacenik then stared with incredulity, well you will have heard it all before, no, my precious one?

SONG FOR THE SPIRIT OF NATALIE GOING

qui s'est réfugié
ton futur   en moi
—STÉPHANE MALLARMÉ, *"A Tomb for Anatole"*

Small bundle of bones, small bundle of fingers, of plumpness, of heart,
predicate, prescient, standing and wobbling, lit up in the joy,
lachrymose GA, your bundle oh KA, the unfolding begun of the start,
of the toys, of witnessing, silly, the eyes startled and up, re-
énveloped now and fresh with the art, chordate, devoted,
sunk in dreaming of wisps and startled awake—*This is morning.*
This is daddy. This is the number eight—spacey, resplendent,
in seersucker bib, overalled, astonished, in dazzling fix
on the small crawling lights in their spaceship of night and the
plug and the cord and the big one's delight, pausing,
mezzed by mobile HEH HEH and again, stinging the shopkeepers,
the monkeyish mouth, *knees, child knees—need to have the child*
here—absence—knees fall—and falling, a dream, a final
singsong UH HAH in the starkest of suns, the heat now a blanket
now a song of your soul—Such a sharp love there is! Such a loud
love there beats! Such a filled hole you leave, in the dusk in the room,
in the wobbling hours of what has refúged, your future in me.

Natalie Joy Hertel-Voisine, 1994–1995

SHANKED ON THE RED BED

The perch was on the roof, and the puck was in the air.
The diffident were driving, and the daunted didn't care.
When I came out to search for you the lauded hit the breeze
On detonated packages the bard had built to please.

The century was breaking and the blame was on default,
The smallest mammal redolent of what was in the vault,
The screeches shrill, the ink-lines full of interbred regret—
When I walked out to look for you the toad had left his net.

The discourse flamed, the jurors sang, the lapdog strained its leash—
When I went forth to have you found the tenured took the beach
With dolloped hair and jangled nerves, without a jacking clue,
While all around the clacking sound of polished woodblocks blew.

When I went out to look for you the reductions had begun.
A demento took a shopgirl to a raisin dance for fun,
And f'r you, for me, for our quests ridiculous and chaste
The lead sky leered in every cloud its consummate distaste.

The mayors queued for mug shots while the banner rolled in wind
That beat at bolted windows and bore down upon the thin,
And everywhere warped deliverers got bellicose and brave,
When I walked out to find you in the reconstructed rave.

The envelopes were in the slots and paperweights were flung.
When I came down to seek you out the torrents had begun
To rip the pan from handle and horizons from their shore,
To rip around your heady heart looking there for more.

MEETING AGAIN, AFTER HEINE

The moon rose like a blooming flower.
The tin in the hand clattered its charge.
We walked by in the wavering hour,
I looking away, you chattering hard.

Met by luck, with like destinations,
We startled again at what ended in pique.
Strollers out, seeing us, had no notion;
A car alarm cycled its querulous shriek;

Eighth Street sank in the crack of its nightfall;
You pressed your satisfactions on me.
You in your urgency remarked *after all*
Kindling your passions was enmity;

Passions had finally erased your calm,
Made composure a prop of the past.
I mugged that street noise, din, bedlam
Prevented my hearing your story at last.

As I walked home the strollers were thinning,
The moon bobbed above roofs like a ball,
The shade at the bus stop waved to me, beckoning,
And I nodded fast in the fast nightfall.

SONNET OF ALTERNATE STARTS
FOR A POEM OF COMPARISON

These people are cockroaches, a coupla cockroaches.
Those cockroaches kept the town on tenterhooks.
Like bugs, the yokels won't go away.
You cockroaches! Get thee off and how!
Whaddaya doin here, cockroaches, whaddaya say?
Without their creeping, I would have found—
A cockroach might more blameless be, you think?
O ya know daguy's a cockroach by dalook but he—
Like their namesakes, they're drawn to sludge.
Damn the cockroach life upon the lea.
What bug shall I compare with you?
You shittin me, you cockroach mouth.
Anest, the big one hies off the small.
Cockroach yer a fool off the poohbah sled.

RUN ON A WAREHOUSE

What he had said came back to him.
Sectioned seat, sectioned seat.
The lift caught wind and swayed him in.
Big armoire, big armoire.

For some time he had felt it stir.
Sideboard door, sideboard door.
He sashayed through the conifers.
Dad's chair, dad's chair.

He had not known how far he'd come.
The blanket chest, the blanket chest.
A sourceless light suffused the run.
Love seat, love seat.

He had not come for his own sake.
All fixtures new, fixtures new.
Before the end he'd need to break.
Wall to wall, wall to wall.

So buckily he bore his load.
Filigreed frame, filigreed frame.
He could not see the lodge for snow.
Canopied bed, canopied bed.

He'll not forget the moment soon.
Cuckoo clock, cuckoo clock.
Now over snow a glimpse of moon.
Savvy desk, savvy desk.

There were but two things he required.
Glass breakfront, glass breakfront.
The slope was steep and he was tired.
Just a hutch, just a hutch.

FRACTURED FAIRY TALE

So activate then. Beforehand the birds
settle in for a roost, and the shiny clock hands
start to rattle. The frog prince bewails
his casaba schnozz. *De*-activate's more like it.

Several men rest their rakes at their crotches and begin to talk.
They are having an ur-argument. They are arguing over
pure and impure analyticity, or error theory or a nonfactualist
theory about ethics. It might be the Chinese Room Argument.
The light through the elms reminds them of dinner.
The hunger reminds them of loss.

DOZE DOLL DOES WIZ BIZ—a century that, her sleeping,
a stenotic century self-circling, noodling its tunes, drug
by the scruff, its kitchen, to stand, squinting, at *thing*
coherent, drooping from clouds, bungeeing to boot.

THE VIEW FROM THERE

The old boss was surprised when you ran into her
on the street. Behind her eyelashes a model TV
hummed a sports coach and a car. The old boss
said, for instance, *Well I'm so glad things are going
well for you* with genuine surprise. She rubbed
at her eyelid and tried to revise her history of you,
invisibly. But it showed. The lazy sky and the car
gliding under the trees, the library's false front:
the view made a fit backdrop for hysteria.
She thought she was in the clear; she was wrong.

Old patrons know to patronize, the sports star told the
sports coach, although you could not hear him from
outside the store. Herr Arbeit showed me the desk by
appliances: eleven more forms to blot with dry
snow, seven mock beavers to stuff. Then show.
My work is cut out to a tee.

CLOCK RADIO

expunging Ponge

That each second escorts a fresh plash. Slatted awning, rec room wall,
bald black translucence, the numerals—flip. The methodical tumbling
drives it to hum at the pitch it extracts from the wires.

Its cousins in Holland sing slightly higher. Its march it propels with
reluctance. Its drive is for the offbeat, the cack-handed, the apocopated.
It sings with regret for its thrum.

The clock radio strives to become its grandfather only with
ambivalence, spilling its pool on the nightstand with a modesty and
steadiness in the clicks of its onerous job, in the particles that sworl in
its wake.

CHOSEN

Under tubed lights the blue light
pounds and pounds.
Bartleby's ghost in an assiduous swoon

pricks my buttons, three, four, six—
collars me forward, a punk at toil,
regurgitates a scrod fish bone,

—*So do I! But I didn't know it had a past tense*—
waves the cut, a blotto
mohel uncapped, a singing sevens without

position, listens in to *splices of my pride,*
hies Hesiod's map o faithfully,
switches offices when my back is turned.

He yells at me in Norse. Over and again
the instructional stews
confounded me. And see the brethren's back.

Earn it. What? Had he a pfennig to
call his own he'd bail.
Or rather I'd unhaunted be—I'd *haunting lack.*

Above the blue light a stippled moon creaks into place
and, in the dark,
the macro cuts a three-span wheel for a ten-palm cart,

the button bar masticulates, the wavy mind
waves off in space.
Bone collating—now *that's* a job.

SOURCE CODES

SELF AND ATTRIBUTES

When the wind shifts, the dirt—uh, earth—kicks
up. It skirts the pages of the catalogues

that line the steel link, it scarifies the retina, it
scumbles up the new gas line in Mr. Rodriguez's

RV. I see you levitate before you risk the
plunge. Swinging into the western blast, the screen

door sings although the brothers oiled it—gone
to flaxseed, gone to hay—afore the late moon dis-

appeared. The crux is alive at the fork of me, in
a particulate breeze that rakes. *Ai-ay-ai-ee*

the prairie hums, *ai-ay-ai-ee*—as if this filtering
dandled, upswung thing could hear it sing,

as if the particles of the earth were populate,
as if each trailed a self in the whining wind,

—*what?* the self that is you interjects. *Let's
get the roadside back in view.* It's just Lester's

daft mutt Seagram's grave the winds kicked
up. He'd had him spayed cockeyed is how it's

told, and ever doting dug him there. We reassert
the selves but the Seagrams of the earth they

sift us with silt no mind our gear in a wind that takes
going off to heart, or what heart a silt self has

in the greater earth it constitutes. *Go get the truck*
you say and then the band picks up.

FIVERS

A man
walked into a
bar carrying his sheaf
of poems. *Whaddaya have,* the bar
keep said.

The man
had had it with
drink. *An audience would
help,* he whined, and the bar's patrons
rushed for

the loo.
*Let me give you
a slice of advice,* the
bar keep said. *Lay low—memorize
your best*

*and when
they least expect,
shoot.* The man creased his sheets
on the bar, damned his memory.
It's shot

to shit,
he said. The keep
turned back to polishing
his glasses and thought, *enough with
advice.*

A man
with a hat the
size of Cleveland strode in —
Not another one. The other
drinkers

returned
to the bar from
the john. *Whaddaya have*
and the hat said, *Glenfiddich. Neat.*
Now that's

a good
patron, the keep
said to the man who was
at his own verse, distraught. *Note well.*
You won't

see a
better. Drinkers
clumped about the hat like
batter on a spoon. A man left
a bar

with his
sheaf of poems.
Harder and harder it
gets to stay sober, harder and
neater.

PRODUCE, PRODUCE

after Frost

The thinnest meal on the slightest isle
Sustains but poorly. So: the file
Of men and women, mile and mile,

In consult with the wizened bat.
Plumes and boas're where it's at —
She won't remember saying that.

If hunger takes them to the coast,
They find a spectacle to toast.
Or several of their peers to roast.

Those that make it to the south
Are lucky to live thumb to mouth.
They might prefer the Catamount

Where greenish mountains freeze the nuts.
Though scavenging is an art that's bust
The ravenous can be beauty sluts.

Those lucky few who do adduce
The food that keeps them from the noose
Will crave on, too. Produce, produce.

EVERY LOVER ADMIRES HIS MISTRESS

Every lover admires his mistress

eyes
looks like a squis'd cat
awry
heavy
mammis
two double jugs
she have filthy
breed lice
very monster
dowdy
obscene
he love her once

errors or imperfections of body or mind, Ipsa haec delectant
lover admires his mistress, though she be very deformed of herself
a swollen juggler's platter face, or a thin
have clouds in her face, be crooked
mammis, her dugs like two double jugs
that other extreme, bloody-fallen fingers
she have filthy, long unpared nails
back, she stoops
very monster, an oaf imperfect
dowdy, a slut
obscene, base
he love her once, he admires her for all this

every lover admires his mistress
ill-favored, wrinkled, pimpled, pale
having a swollen juggler's platter

clouds in her face
be crooked, dry, bald, goggle-eyed
looks like a squis'd cat, hold her
eyed, black or yellow about the eye
hook-nosed, have a sharp fox-nose
simo patuloque, a nose like a prom
uneven, brown teeth, beetle-browed
over the room, her nose drop winter
her chin, a sharp chin, lave-eared
awry too, pendulis mammis, her dugs
in that other extreme, bloody-fallen
nails, scabbed hands or wrists, a
she stoops, is lame, splay-footed
waist, gouty legs, her ankles hang
breed lice, a mere changeling, a
complexion savours, an harsh voice
virago, or an ugly tit, a slug, a
boe, a skeleton, a sneaker (si qua
ment looks like a mard in a lanthorn
world, but hatest, loathest, and
thy nose in her bosom, remedium amor
a scold, a nasty, rank, rammy, filth
obscene, base, beggarly, rude, fool
Thersites' sister, Grobian's scholar
for all this, he takes no notice of
or mind, Ipsa haec delectant, veluti

have her than any woman in the world

Text taken from Robert Burton, The Anatomy of Melancholy

THE PROMISE OF STEUBEN

> There is a crack in everything.
> That's how the light gets in.
> —LEONARD COHEN

I wish I had a Packard for every time you stopped.

A child climbs through the glass of the storefront with
a hold on his mother. Hoppy sights one and dips into
housewares. The shouts pepper screeches as the wagons
brake fast. Radios hum Hawkins' revenge at top blast.

D.C., mid-century. IBM's motto is THINK,
Brasilia's seats girdled with an op-art design.
In the sheets of hot currents, in the particulate summer,
in the humming headbashing heat and in god,
the children lay down in the project's sweet gleam,
in a room blinking red from the out-bubble turning,
the girl spooking the boy with her moving and quakes,
the boy waiting in safety for sleep, or for Mom.
You don't have to be Jewish to love a lay-dreaming.

Hoppy's in his do-rags, the boy tries for a touch
and the kitchen's a cartoon, Hoppy a green dog,
the do-rags no longer, a mouse swooping in, cape
slapping, jaw fixing the boy, a "beady" eye too—
the mattress is wet with this small boy's sweating,
my buttons are wrong with our small boy's waking,
Jack Paar's newest set has fronds behind, waving,
and here in the marigolds on the traffic isle fronting
the sleek Golden Mile and its wan Piggly Wiggly
pancakes are flipped by a sedulous cook in that heat-
wave just mid-way through a century's detritus:
Fallingwater, Mies, a Texaco glass.

The Danes did it right, *plop plop*,
the wind on my skin, *fizz fizz*,
in the showroom it gleams *I can't believe*
a perch for McHale, *I ate*, for Have Gun, for Hoss.
A pitcher of teak, a bee in the glass, a deck
wrapping the house with a tree up its neck,
and I helped, you see, I helped with the
waves, with the flickers that fell and the
buckets of wheat that poured from the drapes—
while you're dusting, I raved.
The boy is squinting at the swirls on the wall
and counts the repeats to the highest, fourteen,
while Hoppy looks out at him, tapping his foot
like a speed demon on course to orbit with kids.

I lied about D.C. I lied about stores. It's a
waiting room missing its untoward fores, it's a
dog's shaking off after a dip in the lake, it's the
mad, mad come fly that makes the schlong stiff, it's
Doodlebug and Pickles and Fireplug's riff.
From the flower the zoom out to outerspace speeds.
Rod intros honeymooners and a jukebox
a-fritz. Late Dorsey. With Ed.

The boy's in his lair and the boy is alone, as he sparks,
as he sparked in the arms of a white man he shone,
as he will when he sparks in a lockout to come.
He's a radio. He's a tornado. No dough.

He's got a big one, size of a A-bomb torpedo.
The Danes could arrange for the passions to rise
and the settings not inflame, not quell, not haze
but in utter placidity backdrop the throes.
The boy swats the light. He's sparking. He's right.

HAND-ME-DOWNS: THE MOVIES

Power schmauer. The trees glinting their crystal boughs beyond the
    breakfront
Wave on, unconcerned at the perilous act the speaker and her cronies
    consider.

A tricolor wager hits the felt, its paper rustling, its androgynous scent
    stirring
The air of its daring. The tuxes demur. Flutter the molls. The runner
    stands

Clean out of the way as the goose V en route to Bahamadian skies
    breaks
And wheels in the skylight. Dumb schmo. In the days when they made
    films,

Real movies, like with a camera store employee charged in a theft and
    then
Slaughtering, "butchering," the old woman—or with the lug
    discovering

His date is black via her hipster brother—or with the Engels recitation
    beside
A heap of junk, back then, yea, we cut some real corners. Cold
    Mountain's

Incline rolls rocks big as words; Maya; a bloom; and a forehead. A cold
Bucket dipper in a cold high stream. Juncos light on the air conditioner

Shell of the room where the molls are powdering. How can gills really
    propel

Them past a pate or two holding forth at the rum punch? His
    interjected *Gills?*
Propel? stole the thunder. The trees stirring their sharp twigs ice up in
    the spot,
Like fingers on currency, or chips. In the 70s, power counted for
    rocks—

For bread—strewn on the walk, from the embankment the swooping of
    birds.
Scrims of six-legged creatures blew out behind poems. Saucered, the
    tea,

Gunpowder, sloshes, as the girl, pie-eyed, peppers her father with kisses
Until Mabel in the pumpkin cries through Harrod's, though louder be

The lift chimes overdubbed. Red poppies had dibs—although, as we
    say,
"Metaphorically." The gowns glinting in front of the breakfront move

Characteristically. Gowns, they should. Can't someone explain to her
The sparkling allure of the wager and the winning streak? On your
    mark—

BENNY THE BEAVER: MY FATHER'S TALE

Benny's tail would only drum.
All day while fellow beavers drug

The tree limbs to the riverbank
Benny slapped his tail to bang

A beat on hollow logs,
Keen for external analogs

To the hums within his head.
Benny's folks despaired. *Hey*

Wisenheimer shape up or else —
Else he chose and so was helped

Clean off to military camp.
Would it cure his cooking

Beat from manifesting in-
Appropriately? Some feat. If

Benny tried, it didn't show.
All day long, his tail did shake

And set up such a strapping quake
The slaving campers riled. Quod

They: Benny's antics are not fair!
We'd love to lolligag on air,

Drumming for sheer sound alone.
Camp authorities thought alike

And banished Benny from the dam.
Dizzy, mournful Benny, damned

To wander up the mountainside,
Thought himself worthless. So

At the top he fixed to plummet off
The tip. Above the treeline odd

Silence fell. His footfalls each were bombs.
When suddenly up from far below

A curdling yell that seemed to make
His name. *Benny!* Did he hallucinate?

The trappers are coming! Benny,
Set to! What's needed's a bang,

A racket by you! And Benny complied.
With his tail he raised a cacophony

That sent the traders highing tail,
Their bejesus out. *Hail Benny the Beaver, to*

Him We Owe All! And indeed, they did.
The Benjamin School for Drumming

Draws the best of beavers to study
Drums. And Benny? He's dead.

On an upper story, someone is dying.
On this lower floor, I am revising.
Throw the dead ones out. They rise.
The loved ones retire. They cry.
Isotopes, pockets, dragonflies, bread:
How can I indemnify the dead, long gone on my aperitifs?
They have brought nothing but grief.

*

Set it off on the left, oh, set it off on the right, now, set it off.
Though the circle's closed and the sacrament is had, lo, set it off.

The collars of reprieve, the pendulous aggrieved, do sadden now.
Once the deed's replayed and merriment displayed, they sadden, how.

Flowers on the left, oh, flowers on the right, now, bow you down.
Though the circle's rent and the birthday bottle's spent, they bow down.

*

It is my work that waits, not yours.
It is my clock that ticks, not hers.
I have reason to undertake an expiry report.
The dead will die nigh, nonetheless.

*

August. The beat of the firefly
In its bleep of light

Across the dark lawn.
An indigent woman stares   and sips.

*

There was a woman,
She was dying.
When I denied her,
I was lying.
Her face it was a
Piteous kite
That hovered o'er
That butterfly,
That blighted spirit
Gone tonight.

*

Remove what is of consequence—the nine yards whole: the homonym,
Beneath the skull the tender tent of clavicle prone,
The diffidence, the sailor's knot, the sickle cell, the humanate,
The bone that breaks, the outer clotted artery she bent.

*

'Night. 'Night. A lawn that exhales insects, grass. A

Chute in which the elevator
Shudders up. A wave, a kiss, a token

Spliff. Another time, it was, when you were here &

Harping on our pockets' pilling,
Wary. Receive me though I have arrears

To each lector at the lectionary.

AIR MAP

The grid, west of Lincoln, Nebraska, could be
Agnes Martin's: all purplish white,
marked with hatching, Richart chocolates in
a box—some squares ribbed, some chenille,
checks close-cropped like a flat-top crew,
some wavy orbs, some purled, some knit,
some bisected by blue hypoteni,

until the white quilt bunches up in sun,
purple shadows blue, bluer in retreat,
stream snaked like a rip in a Reebok welt,
chunk coral's white spines of trilobites,
Rayogram leaves in negative, Abyssinian's
mussed fur post-grooming's blue rinse.

Dwellings must be there but god knows where:
a field dog cuffed by an impatient man,
a truant pouring a cup of gin, a woman
leaning into her hand until her stiff side swells.
From here, it's all a flat board hatched
for a ghost's game on the earth's odd rim.
Reflected from the wing as we lunge over,
veins glint silver and mute again.

Then: brown and moss shot with threads
on the checkered body of the globe. This
body's old: the bloom is off. It folds and scabs,
ribbed like a Lhasa apso, trussed, mossed
forest blisters on a walnut moult. Now
orbs, stripes, chutes are Missonis in an earth-
toned year or, beneath brown gauze, Twister,

Bridget Rileys or make-up palette a giant
lost—what's lugged in getting there!—
west, only to cross back again—
the clouds too clotted to release the grid or,
summering, the grid a gaudy green.
What is left behind—bagels, screen—what—well—
suffice—shores the variegated field of what is between.

GUEST + HOST = GHOST

after Duchamp

The drive in the night's lit by lightbulbs looped
into cows, then chiles, then stars;
it's late in the century when Calhoun arrives
and, on foot, on the front stoop, rings.

Oh, Cal has the prettiest groom in the sea,
Oh Cal has formidable ch'i.

Bettina busses Cal and leads him inside
where revellers turn red and gold
in raising their duck to the pal of their Fred,
the prettiest groom in the sea.

At midnight the Andersen windows slide back
and, singing the syne, the troupe
finds Calhoun redoubled in the dank moonlight
to join his Fred in the brine.

Oh, Cal has the prettiest groom in the sea,
Oh Cal has formidable ch'i.

The glass that is etched with his lament
is repro'd upon this card.
Go gently (my love!) in the chocolate mills
that compass your own shipyard.

SLEEPING SISTER

Stop spackling for a minute and listen to me.
I had a dream, and you were its Eve.
The room was leaden from the radiation,
The moths on the curtains put up a racket,
He called himself ironing but his arm was limp.

You were more of a vaporous lug, a scheming;
Your varmints—they were yours—double-did
The hall, while the beach waves sound increased
And his hair became your hair, and when he turned—

The avenue at seven is lit like a steel pit.
Still streets, a fire in the sky, bus slow.
Ah, temptress, for that extra sly iamb!
I wanted you so, then, I wanted you so.

CASSIUS

Do not fell the smallest to spare the tallest.
Do not braid with umbrage the hair of repose.
Do not trifle with holy expectations.
Do not make of me an exception.

Do not bargain fast the last of it.
Do not gentle go within that tower.
Do not splay the legs or tend the sour.
Do not make of me an exception.

Do not fail the one who loves you most.
Do not recognize the incognito.
Do not milk the sow of introspection.
Do not make of me an exception.

QUINCY IN LAGOS

LAGOS, Nigeria, July 9—Nigeria's military ruler tried
to calm an angry nation tonight, after the sudden death of
the opposition leader, Moshood K. O. Abiola, by agreeing
to let outside experts take part in the autopsy.
—ROGER COHEN, The New York Times, *July 9, 1998*

The bog-man's stippled in celluloid, grist for the mill.
The Mohican is Irish now on-screen, his father a shill.
I've gone to the meadow,
I've come back in loss.
The wails of the widow,
the brass of the boss.

Quincy's props man packs the sham socks, he whistles this song.
The airport in Lagos teems over, the reception's all wrong.
We sing what we know of,
we singe when we try.
The poster head glowing
against a dumb sky.

How did we know what we see, when we saw through the mind?
What citizen without cummerbund could Columbo yet find?
What mourning is mete grief,
what picture is true?
The raveling of relief,
the singing eschewed.

LEDGER

Having been a tenant long to a rich Lord;
Not thriving, I resolved to be bold,
And make a suit unto him, to afford
A new small-rented lease, and cancell th' old.

—GEORGE HERBERT, *"Redemption"*

They did not understand that even an economic world order
cannot be built on merely economic foundations.

—ARNOLD J. TOYNBEE, *A Study of History*

LOSS LIEDER

It's an icebox
missing freon,
elevator
that's kaput.
It's a danger
in the stashbox,
fast upon us
citigrade.
Lay your head
on radiators,
drive the needle
through the vein;
I'll be here when
you're no longer,
opal midnight
my refrain.
I'll sing it when
you're mentioned
if the cost is
not too great,
and if I haven't
met you coming
toward us
in the haze.

THAT BEEN TO ME MY LIVES LIGHT
AND SAVIOUR

Purse be full again, or else must I die. This is the wish
the trees in hell's seventh circle lacked, bark ripped by monstrous dogs,
bleeding from each wound. We see them languid there,
the lightened purse a demon drug. *Less, less.*

At the canal, the dog loops trees in a figure eight—
a cacophony of insects under sun. A man against a tree nods off.

Let there be no sandwich for the empty purse.
Let there be no raiment for someone scint.
Let blood run out, let the currency remove.
Let that which troubles trouble not.

My father in the driveway. Legs splayed behind him. Pail beside him.
Sorting handfuls of gravel by shade and size. One way to calm
a pecker, compensate for stash. *Dad!* I lied.

The man shifts by the tree and now grace is upon him.
The slant of sun picks up the coins dropped by travelers and—lo!—
grace enables him to see. The demon dog fresh off an eight barks, too,
standing, struck by the man, by the coins, barks at their glare;
the man reaches in scrim at the glint in the light and thinks *Another
malt.* The flesh is willing, the spirit spent,
                                    the cloud passes over—
relief is not what you think, not the light. Regard the barking
dog now tugging at the dead man's leg becoming bark.

You be my life, you be my heart's guide,
you be the provision providing more,
you be the blood—stanch the sore!—

you be failing

                    proportion (mete) . . .

Steward of gravel squints up at the girl who is me.
What?, defensively. Out of the east woods, a foaming raccoon spills.
Palmolive executive? Palmolive customer? Palm's stony olives
                    on the embankment of limestone or soapstone or
shale. Leg of the man clamped in the dog's mouth. Mouth
of the man open and unmoved. Voice of the man:

Three dolls sat within a wood, and stared, and wet when it rained
into their kewpie mouths. They were mine to remonstrate to the
trees at large, the catalpas and the fir, the sugar maples in the
glade turning gold. To each is given, one doll began, so I had
to turn her off. Consider how it was for me —

Flash of the arrow and the foam falls down. Three balletists
ignoring pliés bound onto the long lawn and its canalward
slope. I am underwater and they haze in the light,

                                        mouth

but do not sound. In the arrow's blink they start.

Decimal as piercing of the line—
Table as imposition of the grid—
Sum as heuristic apoplex—
Columns in honeysuckle cents—or not.

Just this transpired. Against a tree I swooned and fell, and
water seeped into my shoe, and a dream began to grow in me.
Or despair, and so I chose the dream. And while I slept,

                                                    93

I was being fed, and clothed, addressed—as though awake
with every faculty, and so it went. Then: blaze, blare of sun
after years uncounted, and synæsthesia of it and sound,
the junco's chirp and then the jay's torn caw, arc
of trucks on the distant interstate, your *what the fuck*
and then her call. Beside me, pinned to a green leaf,
in plastic and neat hand, a full account. I had indeed still
lived, and been woke for more. So, weeping then, I rose.

ROANOKE AND WAMPUMPEAG

Child, entering Ye Olde Trading Post, takes the pegs upon the walls
For trees, fingers the beaded doll in buckskin dress, a moccasin,

A square of maple sugar maple leaf, small imprint of a fingernail
In its clear window. She wants the Minnesota charm in green,

Six of ten thousand lakes in silver raised, Babe the Blue Ox and her
Mate. REAL! CAN OF WORMS! a label states; another, on a bow

And arrows stapled into cellophane: APACHE ARROWHEADS,
AUTHENTIQUE. Dread of parents, parked, smoking, in the lot.

Piecework of the quiet shade. Piecework of the whoosh of trees
Blowing beyond log walls, adults murmuring over turquoise rings,

Low radio, woman propped with *The Making of a President*
Open in her hands. The child calculates the thieving odds, balks.

A brother, suddenly. *Come ON*. The dollar buys four old-tyme sticks,
Swirled barber poles in green and brown, horehound-hard and stale,

Each a member's of the family, their car on gravel moving out, trunk
To traders and the totem pole, behind the ghastly, grinning cow.

Child in the thick of yearning. Doll carted and pushed
like child. The aisles purport opportunities —

looking up, the women's chins, the straight rows
of peas and pretzels, Fizzies' foils, hermetic

boxes no one knows. *I'll get it!* What thing therein
— bendy straws, powder blue pack Blackjack gum —

will this child fix upon? On TV, women with grocery carts
careen down aisles to find expensive stuff. Mostly,

this means meat. This, then, is a life. This, a life
that's woven wrong and, woven once, disbraided, sits

like Halloween before a child, disguised in its red
Santa suit, making its lap loom the poppy field

Dorothy wants to bed. *Can I have* and the song's begun.
O world spotted through more frugal legs. O world.

EACH'S COT AN ALTAR THEN

. . . from the service of self
alone. . .

grasses in low wind high sun

(streamers of starlings)

Joseph hauling the leg with his hands, corn stubble to stalk, horizon no
house—

Low animal flash in the riot of leg—

all such good works as thou hast prepared for us to walk in

This one request I make if it mean foot or glove
Repair, deplete the debt as I am out of love

carrion   calumny

and come into the field of blade poplars glinting,
leg pulled like a cart on the mule of the man
grasshopper of cropduster sprawled in the sun
desperate pastor all yield   green pan

Limb lost? Likely.
Undone? Likely.

Let us grant it is not amiss

who bears the Count Chocula shipment up
who razors the retractable in the joint
who sings the bass of Anthony
who cries for mercy in the placid field,

far now to go.

to reel the streets at noon —
great weight in his lightness —

So. Bike at door.
On it. Avenue
of the Americas   (against traffic)
a stream.
        The
spareribs hot against
his knees.

fiduciary re
no sib
ability   re-
spond dis
Eisenhower, Eisenhower

                                                                    sty

pend   sur

plus one is
                    x, solve for.   solve

vent

A kind of Mamie-dress, that's right, with the bodice—
no—you'd need darts here first. But that kind
of print—

                    kind of

a clear light above Joseph and his leg and the dry dry stalks and the clatter
    he makes

                    seek a proper return for our labor

CARNIVAL

Boy in lit din—trailing tickets in strings, a man on his hand—
tilts at the red poles, dots, rainbows in kliegs; tilts past

rickety gates manned by bent men, men bent into bars like the man
with the boy bends to bars, too; tilts as a t-shirt shoves and dissolves.

Boy blinking in noise, with coupon trails, veers at the hand out to
Wipeout near Yo-yo and Claw; Graviton, Zipper, Chaos, Rok & Roll—

this: major ride row. Slime Buckets. Orbiter. Night with its
sear of crayon through ink. Boy in the spill of shapes liquid at night.

Motherfucker give 'em to me, the man's the boy's master and
his own dive he feints, bending, too. *This ain't TV*. Pulled up to

concessions. Stopped straight under white. Major Ride Row,
its Fire Ball, Tornado, zipped out of reach, sees the man on the end

of the boy levy a string for a carton of drinks. *It's not free*.
Would that a wave from the night past the trees take him, take him,

far away from me: this they both wish from their roiling seas,
in dins of temptations, in the slugs from the noise both would be.

I was at and about everything, nodding through the mall lot,
cutting through the yard with quick, light steps.

When the rains came,
they left the hillside
and moved to the high ground
where a quilt scrap sustained them
in late, dark readings from
Isaiah, bright
            "and they

regard the objectivity of the market as a disguise for an abdication of
    values and of intellectual dependence"   WM PFAFF, 1981

In this house, objects
operate optimally.
The log on the fire is
seasoned to flame,
the chips in the basket
Olestra cramp not.

        "You're hurting my arm."

—and then the jingle wings in
          —striated penna of the ostrich
               —O noble heart,

ponder thy end.

                              On the floor we saw the pigs
                                 in space routine:
                         Jack whirling in the zigzag of the
                                rise, the fall, the buy high,
                                                   sell.
                    Bodies doubled over slush underfoot
                                        of the tape,
                                    loss-evidence,
                                       white shit.

He got the newsprint spread about
So he ha, so he ha
He got the newsprint spread about
So he ha

the signature inscription, the sport-fuck after boot scoot, the U.S. of

He got the newsprint spread about
An he hacking, spitting low
He expectorating upon the news

Give me that core lone tearing. Rest your head. Put it here.

"It's just routine."

I will be brief.
Upon his death
They felt relief.

A delight exacting

"We may be hungry
but we won't
turn the other cheek"
(SEMBENE, *Guelwaar*)

The night and the stars and the window
The sigh and the gown and the fiddle
The calling to hymn and from sorrow
jumping   gel O

"Let's put the dutiful graduate student thing away, ok? Dazzle as summarily
as the theorists. Our ducks in a row. No ~~wine~~ whine."

At dawn their path
took sea side by the bethel,
up Guinevere
along the Pathmark lot,
through the early fields,

the sun rising red
and hung.

"Thank you, I prefer to stand."

Tyvek Bruce Willis Buffalo Bertelsmann Turtle Wax Tiger Balm
Nickel Cadmium Postgraduate Ice Cube Waldrop
Exile Witness Nike Iowa Snapple Foucault, The Sands
Browning Tradition, Hejinian, Bly—SKU, ADP, BAP
Time-Warner, Ted Turner, The Favorite Poem Project, the Oulipo, the Fed
Independent Cinema, Mrs. B's, Miss Lou, Reds

lemon trees tennis bracelet desert   highway

She had been pinged, like the
pillar in a pinball, by the die
of god. Lit in the klieg of a
sign. Stung by repletion &

furious in sin, a monolith of
infirmity washed clean. A
domino undone by the smear
on its back. Left to contend
in the swale of her city's
choke-weeds and strife, she had
truck in sinew, in tooth
and in tongue, with divinity,
raw. Then it passed.

"Had killed the whole carload of them."

                                        crawed fish

                                                        bone

When you get your job
in the powder factory
I'll macrame your mask.

                              I don't want to spread it around.

Naturally. The finitude of the body! The demands of the soul!
                                    Did you hear about the butter?

The ironic caw of the crows flapping past to the Farmer's Corn—

and salt

and pepa

                                                    Naugahyde
                                                    TV room
                                                    Overhead glare
                                                    Child crumpled in love

Three dollars fifty cents a celebrity magazine, buck fifty a caffè latte on sale.
A twenty and change for a belt with D rings, a fin for the xeroxing and mail.
Seven twenty the lipstick, thirteen coins the handouts, Susan B. a scone, stale.

My consumerism: Rerelease   *India*
                           Rerelease   *India*

India: a meronym of that dark winter, cold, on foot, Chicago, the ta-*da*
    the grace

                .

"You've got the wrong man."

If memory mimed dreaming then I would have you here again.
You would be laughing gem-like, praising Republicans.
Ailing, sipping sours, you would be diffident.
O that your Curwensville had found
A way to harbor you!
And that I hadn't spent the pound
I'd saved to honor you.

                     The plot in the account books
                     The sermon in the billboard
                   The dark night of the statement
                      Mercy in direct deposit

lights on, nobody home

We doctor shoes
attend the dyeing
heel them
save their soles
in Red Bank, New Jersey

.

"Oh, by the way, just one more thing."

They came from a woolly world and they wanted an exact, undisclosed
freedom.
They wore small hairpins and carried their sons close to their chests.
Before they came, they felt they had failed at understanding the outside
and the inside.
What they found was a replica of nature.
What they found was menace recollected in tranquility.
What they found came in small pine coffins.
They were eager to undertake difficulty and they were eager to repel the
consequences.
They wanted danger to have names they knew.
They came from resplendent churches made of wicker.
They roasted hens.

They built shelters, each with an oak plank frame.
They understood that a gathering of hearts meant for—by now!—few
words.

"Take a seat."
"Thank you, I prefer to stand."

MONEY AND GOD

I

In the country of individuation, I struck out
                                                                  like a match

for the gravid coast. After the copper fields,
                                                          the long loops of city cloverleafs,

the squibs in hillsides spouting the netherworld's flames,
the chrome architraves over gasoline pumps,
                                                          signs scrapped up in lead,

and then a lap of colors in the air vault   on the horizon where the
        black spikes spike up

hearing You beside me as a phantom
                                                          cursing the radio's warble,
You almost in sight when I turn to the empty seat,

You rigging
                the fuel pump as it begins to miss,

                                                          and then again alone on
lines at burger trains in the chill, sad outposts
Leer & Leak   wobble head for the window rear

after the accordion billboards
Motel 6 a.c. blink   soap ingot and its waxy paper shell

the scent of my striped shirt wagging up from its pit
slubbering of a mechanic in twilight, one night,
the body—*ghastly thing!*—unprepared for reckoning,

after   Eat a Cup of Coffee
                                         a knuckle's scrape against a deli wall
                                         wild turkey   road crossing
                                         swimming air over radiator

                    leg on a train—polyvinyled seat
                              rank john

after the money ran out
after the wire came in
after humilia—

            humid—

                    the homily, end of the nation—

waters   gilded   reared in the sun along a crinoline shore

struck like a match for the sea.

II

                                              And I want to tell You about the houses,
                                              each house of its kind—clapboard or
stucco or timber, Germanic gingerbread, brick or stone,
their blocks cut smooth and
well-fitting, longhouse of mud with its
                              woven roof—

each had a milky sheen in the afternoon light, whitewash a scrim not of it
but before it, between it and my self, air dunked in milk and the sun—

Or the customs:

                              small figurines in the front windows winking
                              straw stuffed in a man's clothes and set on the porches
                              fiberglass igloos on the lanate lawns

The inhabitants, burly and wild in their cars.
Money
                              no object.

I saw a woman reach into a parcel of leather with metallic clasps and retrieve
the jangling discourse of our nation

                              small caterpillars in chrysalides, arrayed
                                        on their ends, and she offered these
                              to passing motorists, passersby.

A column of eager faces along the roadside at dusk—
A man crying in a park, despite his fierce demeanor—

and I? Done in, missing, hocked at Hocktide. But 'twere
all strange to me. And the hotel too dear.

III

Hell or high water.   *Well, it's the latter. No room for*
the rest of us, let's take the stairs. It's a wallop, learning the delis
won't deliver up here.

Where I had come from, hell *and* high water   fire

and   snow.

               Sarcophagi picnics—where the lost discussed—

                         Cheating the tax collector—

Yeah you and the everloving country said the cowboy, for example,
the spray on his six gallon faint in the sun.
Freesia poured on the tables, dang if it
                         —shut up, we've counted it all and I'm
sick of it now.

Then wheeling out to dominions on the outskirts—
                              red lights, high hopes—
topless skirts' menu: tops, bottoms, *Japanese* or *Russian.*

Interminable billboards—
                         pass the box of Fannie Mae
said Freddie Mac,
               the storm rolled in.

And along that other coast, a longboat carried the crippled souls
bent and twisted into cutouts of the damned, and a wailing trailed
the longboat as it banked beside the man, collector of interest
that he would not confess.

The silo of another moneylender opened,
its wheat now snakes.

A third, awakened by his
servant, found Lucifer
and two steeds black before his mill—

merchants of the future, sellers of time—

For every *buy high*, a seller's low. You were beside me in the
capitol—al—and then You weren't. Vamoosed like a loan shark
after collect. Denominational oligopsony. Brother Luke
and the double entry. Hermes' fluidity. And so I left.

Now the bright expanse yields up to You.

Radiant sea. I said they were chrysalides, what the woman gave—

The house and its drive faced the sea. The table she'd strutted
was meager but hewn to endure, with a shiny cloth cover, a
checkerboard in red.

Behind her the house glowed milken sheen, a blue like bachelor's
buttons under a tangle of green.

The road along the sea was well tended, loose strife lush on the banks
of its gullies.

I was weary with sleeping out, sore on my feet. Each town had opened
on the last like commercials. Cars blinking past, a *whshh* and away.

Purgatory, a man by the road said, *was charged for its upbringing, as was
Baudelaire by his stepfather.*

Others had tables, others were tending. Pungent solvents, ochre jellies.
Casts of hands on doilies of silk. Wing covers. Tree frogs singing for tubas.
White curds. One man spread a trunk with bitters and salt.

And I wasn't the only one walking—the cars, the cars in and out, their
riders at hand and in hand of the tables, but the millers like me were
sampling on foot.

I could not not put this between us, too. Your gifts which I fretted, neck
and neck with the costs. To pay Paul, rob

Robert. An impounded car, no more cash by the wire—

I could not not fault You. Turn from your jars. Ochre substan—
sin of the fallen deepest. Shield to the radiant sea.

V

Crows harangue the crowds here, too. Cars break down.

A slippery soot

settles on the beaches

some nights.

An animal tears into a boy's bones

as though they were boxes of sweets;

the deacon fights with his

supervisor,

departs, released.

Flip side, same coin. But knit, a place for each—
Your gifts, within a breach—

From here, on the north cliff, lean-to'd and wanting in the oncoming
     dusk,

it is difficult to shirk

Your tackle. Right end, left

out. And so I fight—

stars, ready henchmen, pointing—

the sound of water,

down below, lapping—

dive of carrion to the radiant sea.

By

Your banks there would be plenty

so I

turn from them.

.

Walls of the implacable cliff: dry of the nummary sea.

THE DEBTOR IN THE CONVEX MIRROR

after Quentin Massys, c. 1514

He counts it out. By now from abroad there are shillings and real—
Bohemian silver fills the new coins—but his haul is gold, écu au soleil,
excelente, mostly: wafers thin and impressed with their marks, milled
new world's gold the Spanish pluck or West African ore Portugal's

slaves sling. The gold wafers gleam in their spill by the scale.
Calm before gale: what bought a sack a century before almost
buys a sack now; the Price Revolution's to come. A third of a mason's—
a master one's—day's wage funds the night's wine, Rhine, for his crew

after a big job wraps up. As for dried herring, his day's wage would buy
fifteen mille for a big do; his workers, just nine—18 stroo. Calm in his
commerce is the businessman, and his wife, their disheveled shelves:
she turns a page; her hands are in God but her gaze is on ange-nobles

and pearls, weights and gold rings—one florin in pan, one in his hand.
What sync they are in: calm their regard, luxe, volupté leur mien.
Fur trimmings on jackets, gemstones on fingers—while the
debtor in the mirror has spent what he has on the red hat he's in.

Prayer book illumined: luxury *that*, and to ignore: only more.
Calmed by the calculation of interest, though the figure's been
clear for a good quarter hour, the moneylender withholds it and waits:
the debtor is better with fuzz in his head. In truth, *he*'s distressed: cares

like the shield impressed in the écu dint the meet of his brow
beneath the red hat. What's he reading? Or faking? Caught in the
curve of an office's alarm, an anti- to crime, a drugstore's big boon
long centuries to come, the debtor—about to receive knell to what

peace he might otherwise recall—worries his page. Ability for
reading silently may not be his; the lender's wife puts him to shame,
though the shame in this is the least of his shames. In the yard
beyond her waits one of his lienors for the gold of another.

Schoolmarms ahoy. Scrap history, the parable, the prayer of the
illustrated hours she trembles to hold. He's got his gold, she's mes-
merized or not by its sheen, the debtor's lost to our reflecting of him—
but it's without, a measurement is made—a figure's gesture on the

gravitate street, the fury of a face *in its face*, behind the door ajar, the
fingers of the lienor demarcating fast the size of a peck or a pecker
not so. *The debt is as large as a giant's back turning, large as*
a vulcanic forge. And

                      fragment of the debt imbursed—

                                        size of its toy—

intense regard.
Fume individually, fume

borrower, clipper, catcher, coiner, getter, grabber, hoarder, loser, lover,
    raiser, spender, teller, thirster—

                            scrivener lays out upon collateral, but
what has the red-hat? Zero

                                      and then sum.

So *here* you are.　　　　　　Master.

These ideas,
said Friedländer, were "common possession, freebooty, fair game."

A painting by Jan van Eyck eighty years before Massys', glimpsed
and described in Milan but now lost, was its model: banker and wife;

the portrait of Giovanni Arnolfini in a red hat not unlike Massys' debtor and,
a year earlier, Arnolfini and his wife at their marriage, we know. In the latter,

the self van Eyck daubed in its own convex mirror (one of four figures),
affixed like a crucifix on the backdrop of wall, rides the conjoined hands

as a charm. But nothing foreshadowed the hand of your own.
Your painter's (nineteen, set off for Rome with the jewel of his art)

hand in the gem of its bulge, the hand the pope pronto kissed
with commission—a job, you note, never come through.

Genre derives from the devotional: beauty and *ange* on one side,
deformity by vice on the other, or so said Friedländer. He found the wife's gaze

full of dispirit, "lofty sadness." She and her husband are yes tight-lipped.
The palm of the hand, like the open mouth, were Massys' registries

of emotionality, he wrote, but the souls in this painting have neither.
Sentimentally, it *pleases* Massys "to feel sorrow, and grief takes on

mild forms." Worry's otherwise: Massys's St. Anthony, elsewhere,
tempted by courtesans, peaks his brows—wild, broken peaks!—same as

the moneylender's debtor. So much for effects, effects of Massys,
virtuoso, whose pyrotechnics, "new wine poured into old bottles,"

welled "from a kind of nervous energy—in any event, not from the heart."
"The antithesis of artist" (Friedländer, still): this, the debtor to Leonardo,

to van Eyck, may well have known, knowledge well welling his brows in the
mirror the moneylender ignores.   *My guide in these matters is your self,*

your own soul permeable by beauty,   and mine not,
not even by the swirling of facts, leveling—

                                        how far, indeed,

can the soul *swim out through the eyes and still return safely to its nest?*
That it be

possible

            I cannot leave. Though around me, and the art,

I fail.

                            Thérèse
was the lookout. She watched the cashier in the convex mirror, and I
watched Jean Shrimpton on the point-of-purchase long before it had
its name.   Thérèse:

careful, Catholic, pregnant and smoking.

lips   lipstick

I took the

cylinder in my fingers and slipped it to Christmas.   Thérèse: to the racks,
Seventeen, Tiger Beat. A few moments more and we'd be through the
door.

Maybe it was *in* the painter's hand, *out for a dole*
—so close with Clement's promise!—
that he sought a soul.

And these coins, fragments of a web—

Mary sat and did not labor, despite her Martha's sting.

It's still, tonight. The peepers, out, self-
restrain.
Sometimes a welling up: I've lost
thought in images. Night: a blank.
The stars just stars.
The sternies prick like whin.

Kid's bicycle on its rim, under the road lamp chill
                    as ice.
A soul could be blank as these bald things.
                    Are blank. Or so we thought.

So this much we have: banker and wife, waist-up at table, she
with her prayer-book watching the gold coins spill on the surface

before us. What we see in their clothes is the waist-cinch:
her red seamy bodice, his jacket, furred collars and cuffs.

Behind them, just two shelves: account books and objects—
then, out a window or door, two figures obscured but for

faces and heads, one forefinger and thumb in a U.
In the fore of the table, a diverging mirror, gold frame,

askew. And, by his reflected place, we see, we viewers,
sitting right where we are, a red-hatted man who holds

a book to his chin as though he is sunning. Rather,
he's reading—or trying, by the fold in his brow.

Real light, long, late-day, slants through the window
above him where a steeple's filigree's revealed. And that's all.

Most agree the red-hatted reader's the painter; it matches
his portrait from Wiericx's engraving. The clothing's

outdated, the banker's wife's bodice derives from the portrait
van Eyck did of his wife Margaret in that weird hornèd hat.

And Saint Eligius, patron of goldsmiths, converter of Antwerp,
in Christus' scene, had a curved mirror turned toward outdoors.

Copies of Massys come later. They drop the debtor, insert a
messenger. Imitators of Massys update

                                        the coins.

Not
    that the convex tondo, inside of a painting, was not a dozen a dime —
        not just Massys, not just van Eyck, it was *in the wind* blowing,
      in Brabant, in Ghent, Bruges, Anvers, through the Burgundy hold,
               fresh off a pub's haul and into the workshop,
        popping up through the guilds   ghastly cliché it was then.

But
    we get   ahead   rewind   to the Lowlands   begin.

Astonishing city. A rube, let's say Charles, onions in sacks slung on his
mule's back, he a standout in his coarse sayette, enters this Antwerp,
inhales as he draws near the docks. Gulls swoop; three Fuggers, capitalists,

in wool dickedinnen, speaking abreast in deliberate tread, stop him
cold crossing his path. Street stalls of changers, merchants with money;
crates unloading—fish, sugar—by Spaniards and Danes;

dragomen emitting unrecognizable tongues: such swirl over Charles
in our genre-esque scene. In the movie, we'd hear the THX *clok*,
hooves in their wary trades forth. What little Charles knows of this place

he has heard at the fairs in the mediant towns outlying the western Ypres.
On the way, there'd been Ghent, its self-satisfied sense. Talk there of
trade throttled by this guild or that, trade nip-and-tuck against Bruges':

*Antwerp, said an oiler in Deinze, up-and-comer is it, if you want one
that is. Hub of all nations, market of kings. Nothing there, either,
to stand in the way of a man with ambition or a star in his bush.*

No, if you're smart, you'll go there and quick. Charles had nodded
and drunk from his mug, but the notion then planted by the man
took root. Now, in the pitch of the persons, in the roil of the merchants,

Charles sees there the commerce: purposeful, restive, serene—
a trade's unselfconsciousness, a self-sufficiency in such—
and Charles is impressed. His own small purse, pendant in his

pocket, feels slight but sufficient to one.

                                        Anna Bijns, the young lady
says to him not three days later. She's forthright as a slip, and at once
he wants the pocket fuller, a past that's not his. A girl of means, she—

she could show him her whole shelf of books, her writing-room, her
verses that denounce the psalm-sop, Luther. *Like his sins are
worse than ours,* she'll say, to those more worthy of answer.

"Town common to all nations," Guicciardini later wrote of the city.
"First 'capitalist' center . . . in the modern sense," wrote Chlepner.
When Charles and Massys shared Antwerp its reign had just begun;

each week brought scores of foreigners, folded in like butter,
out to let a household kept kempt in local fashion, clean,
its Dinanderie in order and its linens boiled and hung.

Down Gulden street, the house that's held by the Hanseatic corn
market; across the way, the square that will become, in a score of
years, the world's first stock exchange—shops, fragrant with

Portuguese spices, beckon with the latest haul. The merchant
moneylender leans to the obsolescence of his coins—the paper
debts he trades more in leave gold to the unconjoined, sole

debtors like this painter worrying his paper text. *Livre tournois*,
the French would call them, units of money valued at a Roman
pound, and *livre, book*: not the first time the two are confused.

Charles, counting his ducats, catches a red hat from the *coin*
of his eye, costume of a century before: it's Massys he sees.
The painter's off to work in the salt crusted air, preparing

—away from the *shadow of a city, siphon*, you wrote, of the life
of the studio—

his self to be seen.

New York tonight
            boils in its heat wave. The sidewalks
burn soles. Haze like a coat warms up the ones out.   Prague

floods.

      The market's in side-flip. Each day doubling back
                              the day before,
lobbing,
the stalk that holds coral bells tracing its arbitrary round. Perhaps
the U on the street
                  is a score.

                                    Principal export:

ask Bernays, *he'll* know.   Buy low.

The painter in the mirror wants privacy, not this call that invades
the reading of a book. Your own looked out at us, but mine, *Massys*—
disingenuous, masquerading, stressed and damp—doesn't; weightier
things on his mind he's got not. But he only pretends to absorption.
It's we who discern the privacy he wants, we who can see
what he lacks. It's as though we're instructed to trust the lender,
his own fix being more, well, *sequestered*.
The last century mined focus as a notion, and even here in Manhattan,
a delirium of sorts swabbing its streets,
we tread with the intensity of hounds,
plugged into our earpiece conjointments, or collecting loose change
off of cuffs. Massys' grimace underdramatizes our lot.

thassright, that's what makes genres —
pink ribbon, blue bob —

thaler for the watched fob.

No, thalers   come later.

                                        Not much, you prig.

Later enough.

So the grasping soul is unredeemed. *Freak accident —*
yeah, guy goes up a hill in thorns, ends up on a stick.
Not quite, not impaled, more tacked up.   *Yeah.*
And the grasping soul goes clean.

                              Maybe it's our internalness
we're stuck on.
                              O Captain Me, O Consciousness.
The soul *negotiates* its right of way,

                    O consciousness,

but not without a bargain struck with*out.* Why all
or nothing, is what Charles thinks, watching the painter disappear

O Captain Me

     in a costume fit to paint.

            After all, Charles

knows not the painter's destination.

          In a cloud left by dusty wheels, he

       O captain me, o

hears a boy call *natura naturata! Red (Flemish) herring!* —
and wells with tears. Impossible   *o consciousness*
that this he heard, silt eyes silt ears

     Copper's up

in an older voice, murmuring, away — strange songs of spring that reach
  the rube in worsted wraps, wheels clattering about his self, while
  each breath, immarginate,

clangs to differentiate its action from the world's.

O captain me.
Sad country sack, negotiant, kneels in the dust to pray.

He crams so much in, Massys. *And then I reached*
that time in life when, all my spices scattered, every story turned

                                    lapsarian.

Every surface filled with hardware, pots, jetons—a collector's box—
the world impresses back, impresses with a shield or beast or profile of a noble
    sort—
the same impressions, though the edges of each coin be irregular and bent—
it being half a century before die standardized.
And even then, this penny black with chewing gum, that one having seen
the inside of a shoe, this none but a banker's roll—the analogy

goes grim. Or is it metaphor, what we strive for, we

poets. Book-makers with the odds of slugs.

                       We don't need paintings or / doggerel
                       and on this too you're true.

                 The man hand-making his U in the yard
knows Massys's a kite-man, bad risk, a debtor. All glow and show

   and then off
             world, world, world   with him. Each time

intent to aliment not only he but they

world

what comes his way   gives way.

Even tonight, here, stampede of slugs

in all that enters here, in
pages strewn, in air report and digit-pulse: *his way*. The debtor does not
    know his debt
    to the skittering city. The bank of birds up a skyscraper's flank.
    Patience of his
    creditors. What does a trust in surfaces ensure but faith that the
    surfaces move?

Blue surroundings. Your nose, welling in the car mirror's arc—
my own in the hubcap hull—

What is this but an arrangement of figures on an open field?
But *they overlap*—and this is the *heart*, despite Friedländer,

the heart of the bind of the debtor: a debt becoming due.
Inveigling the day to take orders from *him*—such a ray from the

cathedral, still in construction, for which Massys' metal-work
is said to encircle a well—the red-hatted man pretends.

The soul encumbers what no other soul knows? Think again.
The mirror lies between two scales—one banker's, one maker's—

and Massys is but writ on its glass. It's the man in the courtyard,
the jig up with fingers, who'll reckon the dark fundamentals

once the weigh-ins are done. And the world impresses him, too.

The *world* overlaps them indentures them both.

                                    Car door bangs. Dark Brooklyn, dark
clattering night.

          Though the lineage's strong for the sons of moneylenders,

daughters   don't carry.   They get the short end. *The debtor's excuses*

                                                        are many

for the false fealty of her deals.
    .

               Adept at outline, Friedländer meant. Ready angle of the
               couple's arms, echo of the angle in the glass. Her limpid face
               lit sole. Debtor's histrionics, a painter's joke
    .   shallow as they go.

Car door creaks its opening, back for a pack
of cigarettes. Side mirror loose, door slam. Wheeled overland

                                              from Venice
the Venetian goods—and cotton, from Levant—
are writ up
                  (in the noon sun and portside)

          and certified lading.
The paper suffices for sugar and salt.

CATALOGS OF EXHIBITION

REFLECTED SONNET

A verdant swale appeared to me—
disburthened of perspicacity—
by sunset vaulted o'er. What kine
left the budded quicks will in time
lack the evening star, bedded fast
beyond the gable-wall, and copsed
in barn-light's slumbrous, languid air.

From fane, then, to meet you there,
light glinting through the trees, and moss
soft underfoot, soft leaves, I crost
'til, gleaming in a bower's frame,
in golds, alit, the riverbank,
long light shaking o'er river's glass,
charged me light where now you pass.

for, and after the work of, April Gornik

IN SKY

The high that proved too high, the heroic for earth too hard,
The passion that left the ground to lose itself in sky . . .
—ROBERT BROWNING, *"Abt Vogler"*

The girl is waiting in the room to be discovered.
The girl is attempting radiance.
The girl may be a boy, or vice versa.
The girl is anticipating the man's arrival, later.
The girl is anticipating the man's displeasure.
The girl is anticipating the man's disapproval.
The girl takes no guff.
The girl's mendacity has long been remarked upon.
The girl armors up with *chic*.
The girl carries the blooms, the veronicas, the perovskia.
The girl who may be a boy powders the smalt.

The girl fills the room like smoke.
The girl is a deer in the onrush of lamps, she sits on the planks of the pier.
The girl swings her feet above the surface of the water.

The girl presses out, inhales, still fills her seat not.
The seat is an ink room, not-girl, apprehension.
The girl is mottled with self, with indecision.
The girl's amethyst earrings window her eyes.
The girl twirls her cape before the bull.
She refuses her chest.
She refuses "alabaster."
She refuses your volupty at her expense.

The girl is the hole, the cutout.
The box she is punched from throngs with blue spirits.
The ground is blank as a plum, tank-deep.
O water, O silting of dust. Reticulate.

The room's tonnage sags.
The ground is figure to its own ground.
And she, blade of grass at the Battle at Troy.

The girl refuses the stadium seating.
The girl mixes lazule and vivianite.
The girl was or was not a mother, this is irrelevant.
The girl's skin shelters; her skin burns with self.
At the end of the pier, in the house light, she looks up.
Her shade engulfs her.
The girl's blueism offputs the man.

The Girl look't Blew. Blue funked. Cast indigo.
She yelled bloody blue, she talked a blue streak,
The girl blued her bluebacks on linnets and blue duns.
The girl was waiting to be overtaken.
The girl was cruising for a bruiser.
The girl tilted up at the ciel: blue-domer.
She struck into space like a bolt from the blue.
Azul ultramarino, when I confessed I repented, the girl said.
He was blue mouldy for the want of that drink.

The girl ardent was: ardent, wracked, and replete.
The girl took the retablos from the wall; in her hand its wings shone.
The girl watched, as she listened, the strung lights waver.
The girl's moment for radiance passed.
O she was stippled, O but her room was,
O that the treatment take hold and transform.

The girl swung a gun.
The girl jut her chin fore.
The girl limped with her sidling and stalled.
She has a fast one, it's in a wheel rut, the girl and her blue ruin, gin and her car.
The girl has veined shoulders.
She passes wind.

The girl's form is landmined: flounces, the flesh.
The girl bats the red lock away from her ear.
The girl takes the synapse and invests it with *scene* (insensible sense).
The girl Rapunzel is (NOT). She disdains.

O discrete make me and blocked.
O scurry me forth on the slate patio, and applaud my every squeak.
O I am helpful like a shill (no groin).
Untransmutable plane with your shadowed door.
The room heats like a vise.

The girl splices the water like a seal or a grouper.
The girl's shell grows a rubbery skin.
The girl looks right back, planted.

The girl holds her thumb piano beyond our view.
She, the girl, regards the chimpanzee.
The chamber loses its ceiling and the stars prick through.

The girl breathes. Her sex bucks out of sight.

The girl, blushing: *O did you see me there? Did you?*

for, and after the work of, Susanna Coffey

The author wishes to thank a parcel of extraordinary editors, publishers, and selectors: David Jacobson, Bin Ramke, Lynn Emanuel, Karen Orchard, Robert Hass, Martha Rhodes, Harold Bloom, John Kinsella, Chris Hamilton-Emery, Holly Carver, and Jonathan Galassi.